ADVENTURE AWAITS IF YOU DARE

COLLECT YOUR MEMORIES.
YOUR WORDS. YOUR PAGES.
BOOKS WITH SOUL.COM
COPYRIGHT 2019

ISBN   9781949325652

OUR TRAVEL LOG BOOK

RUN AWAY WITH ME

OUR RECORD BOOK OF 50 AMAZING TRIPS

Bookswithsoul.com
Your Words. Your Pages.

I **WILL** REMEMBER
EVERY **TIME** **YOU**
RUN AWAY **WITH**
ME.

LE**T'S** **RUN** AWAY...

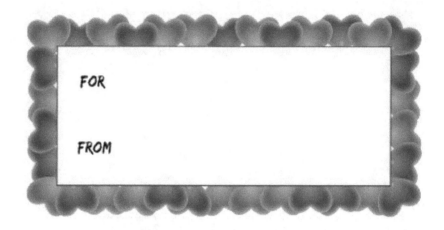

FOR

FROM

IF YOU WANT
TO PRESERVE
YOUR
MEMORIES
YOU CAN

A HISTORY OF US

Let's do it.

We spend our time and money preparing for fantasy trips, weekend getaways, and family vacations we think we will never forget. But unfortunately with time, you forget that adorable man who carried your luggage on his donkey, and the name of that cute little mom and pop hotel with the softest sheets. If you had one book to record the important facts about each and every trip, well…can you say priceless?

Take the time to record your vacations, voyages, road-trips and adventures. Collect and preserve your memories.

In this Travel Log, you can organize and log 50 trips, weekend getaways, and wild adventures:

Section 1:

A section to write down a master list of every adventure you take. If you don't take the time to complete the rest of the book, at least record the date and place of your next 50 trips and adventures.

Section 2:

For each trip, there are two pages with prompts and questions that will help you record important facts and memories. Complete the two pages on the way home from the trip or before you unpack. Make it a habit, and soon you will complete this book with treasured memories. Memories you will remember and pass on to friends, family and even children.

Section 3:

Pages to create a travel wish list, a great reference page, to use when you are planning your next 50 trips.

Here We Go!

50 TRIPS & ADVENTURES

DATE	PLACE

50 TRIPS & ADVENTURES

DATE   PLACE

"THE FIRST CONDITION
OF UNDERSTANDING A
FOREIGN COUNTRY IS
TO SMELL IT."
RUDYARD KIPLING

DETAILS WORTH REMEMBERING

EXPERIENCES WE CAN'T FORGET

WHAT WE ATE

FAVORITE MOMENT OF THE TRIP

DATE- MODE OF TRANSPORTATION

THIS IS WHERE WE WENT!

WHERE WE SLEPT

WHO WE MET

DETAILS WORTH REMEMBERING

EXPERIENCES WE CAN'T FORGET

WHAT WE ATE

FAVORITE MOMENT OF THE TRIP

DATE- MODE OF TRANSPORTATION

THIS IS WHERE WE WENT!

WHERE WE SLEPT

WHO WE MET

DETAILS WORTH REMEMBERING

EXPERIENCES WE CAN'T FORGET

WHAT WE ATE

FAVORITE MOMENT OF THE TRIP

DATE- MODE OF TRANSPORTATION

THIS IS WHERE WE WENT!

WHERE WE SLEPT

WHO WE MET

DETAILS WORTH REMEMBERING

EXPERIENCES WE CAN'T FORGET

WHAT WE ATE

FAVORITE MOMENT OF THE TRIP

DATE- MODE OF TRANSPORTATION

THIS IS WHERE WE WENT!

WHERE WE SLEPT

WHO WE MET

DETAILS WORTH REMEMBERING

EXPERIENCES WE CAN'T FORGET

WHAT WE ATE

FAVORITE MOMENT OF THE TRIP

DATE- MODE OF TRANSPORTATION

THIS IS WHERE WE WENT!

WHERE WE SLEPT

WHO WE MET

"TO TRAVEL IS TO LOVE,
LEARN, AND LIVE
OUTSIDE YOUR SELF."
A.K. SMITH

DETAILS WORTH REMEMBERING

EXPERIENCES WE CAN'T FORGET

WHAT WE ATE

FAVORITE MOMENT OF THE TRIP

DATE- MODE OF TRANSPORTATION

THIS IS WHERE WE WENT!

WHERE WE SLEPT

WHO WE MET

DETAILS WORTH REMEMBERING

EXPERIENCES WE CAN'T FORGET

WHAT WE ATE

FAVORITE MOMENT OF THE TRIP

DATE- MODE OF TRANSPORTATION

THIS IS WHERE WE WENT!

WHERE WE SLEPT

WHO WE MET

DETAILS WORTH REMEMBERING

EXPERIENCES WE CAN'T FORGET

WHAT WE ATE

FAVORITE MOMENT OF THE TRIP

DATE- MODE OF TRANSPORTATION

THIS IS WHERE WE WENT!

WHERE WE SLEPT

WHO WE MET

DETAILS WORTH REMEMBERING

EXPERIENCES WE CAN'T FORGET

WHAT WE ATE

FAVORITE MOMENT OF THE TRIP

DATE- MODE OF TRANSPORTATION

THIS IS WHERE WE WENT!

WHERE WE SLEPT

WHO WE MET

DETAILS WORTH REMEMBERING

EXPERIENCES WE CAN'T FORGET

WHAT WE ATE

FAVORITE MOMENT OF THE TRIP

DATE- MODE OF TRANSPORTATION

THIS IS WHERE WE WENT!

WHERE WE SLEPT

WHO WE MET

"FOR MY PART, I TRAVEL
NOT TO GO ANYWHERE,
BUT TO GO. I TRAVEL
FOR TRAVEL'S SAKE.
THE GREAT AFFAIR IS
TO MOVE."
ROBERT LOUIS
STEVENSON

DETAILS WORTH REMEMBERING

EXPERIENCES WE CAN'T FORGET

WHAT WE ATE

FAVORITE MOMENT OF THE TRIP

DATE- MODE OF TRANSPORTATION

THIS IS WHERE WE WENT!

WHERE WE SLEPT

WHO WE MET

DETAILS WORTH REMEMBERING

EXPERIENCES WE CAN'T FORGET

WHAT WE ATE

FAVORITE MOMENT OF THE TRIP

DATE- MODE OF TRANSPORTATION

THIS IS WHERE WE WENT!

WHERE WE SLEPT

WHO WE MET

DETAILS WORTH REMEMBERING

EXPERIENCES WE CAN'T FORGET

WHAT WE ATE

FAVORITE MOMENT OF THE TRIP

DATE- MODE OF TRANSPORTATION

THIS IS WHERE WE WENT!

WHERE WE SLEPT

WHO WE MET

DETAILS WORTH REMEMBERING

EXPERIENCES WE CAN'T FORGET

WHAT WE ATE

FAVORITE MOMENT OF THE TRIP

DATE- MODE OF TRANSPORTATION

THIS IS WHERE WE WENT!

WHERE WE SLEPT

WHO WE MET

DETAILS WORTH REMEMBERING

EXPERIENCES WE CAN'T FORGET

WHAT WE ATE

FAVORITE MOMENT OF THE TRIP

DATE- MODE OF TRANSPORTATION

THIS IS WHERE WE WENT!

WHERE WE SLEPT

WHO WE MET

"TRAVEL, IN THE
YOUNGER SORT, IS A
PART OF EDUCATION IN
THE ELDER, A PART OF
THE EXPERIENCE."
FRANCIS BACON

DETAILS WORTH REMEMBERING

EXPERIENCES WE CAN'T FORGET

WHAT WE ATE

FAVORITE MOMENT OF THE TRIP

DATE- MODE OF TRANSPORTATION

THIS IS WHERE WE WENT!

WHERE WE SLEPT

WHO WE MET

DETAILS WORTH REMEMBERING

EXPERIENCES WE CAN'T FORGET

WHAT WE ATE

FAVORITE MOMENT OF THE TRIP

DATE- MODE OF TRANSPORTATION

THIS IS WHERE WE WENT!

WHERE WE SLEPT

WHO WE MET

DETAILS WORTH REMEMBERING

EXPERIENCES WE CAN'T FORGET

WHAT WE ATE

FAVORITE MOMENT OF THE TRIP

DATE- MODE OF TRANSPORTATION

THIS IS WHERE WE WENT!

WHERE WE SLEPT

WHO WE MET

DETAILS WORTH REMEMBERING

EXPERIENCES WE CAN'T FORGET

WHAT WE ATE

FAVORITE MOMENT OF THE TRIP

DATE- MODE OF TRANSPORTATION

THIS IS WHERE WE WENT!

WHERE WE SLEPT

WHO WE MET

DETAILS WORTH REMEMBERING

EXPERIENCES WE CAN'T FORGET

WHAT WE ATE

FAVORITE MOMENT OF THE TRIP

DATE- MODE OF TRANSPORTATION

THIS IS WHERE WE WENT!

WHERE WE SLEPT

WHO WE MET

DETAILS WORTH REMEMBERING

EXPERIENCES WE CAN'T FORGET

WHAT WE ATE

FAVORITE MOMENT OF THE TRIP

DATE- MODE OF TRANSPORTATION

THIS IS WHERE WE WENT!

WHERE WE SLEPT

WHO WE MET

DETAILS WORTH REMEMBERING

EXPERIENCES WE CAN'T FORGET

WHAT WE ATE

FAVORITE MOMENT OF THE TRIP

DATE- MODE OF TRANSPORTATION

THIS IS WHERE WE WENT!

WHERE WE SLEPT

WHO WE MET

DETAILS WORTH REMEMBERING

EXPERIENCES WE CAN'T FORGET

WHAT WE ATE

FAVORITE MOMENT OF THE TRIP

DATE- MODE OF TRANSPORTATION

THIS IS WHERE WE WENT!

WHERE WE SLEPT

WHO WE MET

DETAILS WORTH REMEMBERING

EXPERIENCES WE CAN'T FORGET

WHAT WE ATE

FAVORITE MOMENT OF THE TRIP

DATE- MODE OF TRANSPORTATION

THIS IS WHERE WE WENT!

WHERE WE SLEPT

WHO WE MET

DETAILS WORTH REMEMBERING

EXPERIENCES WE CAN'T FORGET

WHAT WE ATE

FAVORITE MOMENT OF THE TRIP

DATE- MODE OF TRANSPORTATION

THIS IS WHERE WE WENT!

WHERE WE SLEPT

WHO WE MET

"TWO ROADS DIVERGED
IN A WOOD, AND I
I TOOK THE ONE LESS
TRAVELED BY, AND
THAT HAS MADE ALL
THE DIFFERENCE."
ROBERT FROST

DETAILS WORTH REMEMBERING

EXPERIENCES WE CAN'T FORGET

WHAT WE ATE

FAVORITE MOMENT OF THE TRIP

DATE- MODE OF TRANSPORTATION

THIS IS WHERE WE WENT!

WHERE WE SLEPT

WHO WE MET

DETAILS WORTH REMEMBERING

EXPERIENCES WE CAN'T FORGET

WHAT WE ATE

FAVORITE MOMENT OF THE TRIP

DATE– MODE OF TRANSPORTATION

THIS IS WHERE WE WENT!

WHERE WE SLEPT

WHO WE MET

DETAILS WORTH REMEMBERING

EXPERIENCES WE CAN'T FORGET

WHAT WE ATE

FAVORITE MOMENT OF THE TRIP

DATE- MODE OF TRANSPORTATION

THIS IS WHERE WE WENT!

WHERE WE SLEPT

WHO WE MET

DETAILS WORTH REMEMBERING

EXPERIENCES WE CAN'T FORGET

WHAT WE ATE

FAVORITE MOMENT OF THE TRIP

DATE- MODE OF TRANSPORTATION

THIS IS WHERE WE WENT!

WHERE WE SLEPT

WHO WE MET

DETAILS WORTH REMEMBERING

EXPERIENCES WE CAN'T FORGET

WHAT WE ATE

FAVORITE MOMENT OF THE TRIP

DATE- MODE OF TRANSPORTATION

THIS IS WHERE WE WENT!

WHERE WE SLEPT

WHO WE MET

"THE WORLD IS A BOOK
AND THOSE WHO DO
NOT TRAVEL READ
ONLY A PAGE."
SAINT AUGUSTINE

DETAILS WORTH REMEMBERING

EXPERIENCES WE CAN'T FORGET

WHAT WE ATE

FAVORITE MOMENT OF THE TRIP

DATE- MODE OF TRANSPORTATION

THIS IS WHERE WE WENT!

WHERE WE SLEPT

WHO WE MET

DETAILS WORTH REMEMBERING

EXPERIENCES WE CAN'T FORGET

WHAT WE ATE

FAVORITE MOMENT OF THE TRIP

DATE- MODE OF TRANSPORTATION

THIS IS WHERE WE WENT!

WHERE WE SLEPT

WHO WE MET

DETAILS WORTH REMEMBERING

EXPERIENCES WE CAN'T FORGET

WHAT WE ATE

FAVORITE MOMENT OF THE TRIP

DATE- MODE OF TRANSPORTATION

_____

THIS IS WHERE WE WENT!

WHERE WE SLEPT

_____
_____
_____
_____
_____
_____

WHO WE MET

_____
_____
_____
_____

DETAILS WORTH REMEMBERING

EXPERIENCES WE CAN'T FORGET

WHAT WE ATE

FAVORITE MOMENT OF THE TRIP

DATE- MODE OF TRANSPORTATION

_____

THIS IS WHERE WE WENT!

WHERE WE SLEPT

WHO WE MET

DETAILS WORTH REMEMBERING

EXPERIENCES WE CAN'T FORGET

WHAT WE ATE

FAVORITE MOMENT OF THE TRIP

DATE- MODE OF TRANSPORTATION

THIS IS WHERE WE WENT!

WHERE WE SLEPT

WHO WE MET

"THE JOURNEY NOT THE
ARRIVAL MATTERS."
T.S. ELIOT

DETAILS WORTH REMEMBERING

EXPERIENCES WE CAN'T FORGET

WHAT WE ATE

FAVORITE MOMENT OF THE TRIP

DATE- MODE OF TRANSPORTATION

THIS IS WHERE WE WENT!

WHERE WE SLEPT

WHO WE MET

DETAILS WORTH REMEMBERING

EXPERIENCES WE CAN'T FORGET

WHAT WE ATE

FAVORITE MOMENT OF THE TRIP

DATE- MODE OF TRANSPORTATION

THIS IS WHERE WE WENT!

WHERE WE SLEPT

WHO WE MET

DATE- MODE OF TRANSPORTATION

THIS IS WHERE WE WENT!

WHERE WE SLEPT

WHO WE MET

DETAILS WORTH REMEMBERING

EXPERIENCES WE CAN'T FORGET

WHAT WE ATE

FAVORITE MOMENT OF THE TRIP

DATE- MODE OF TRANSPORTATION

THIS IS WHERE WE WENT!

WHERE WE SLEPT

WHO WE MET

DETAILS WORTH REMEMBERING

EXPERIENCES WE CAN'T FORGET

WHAT WE ATE

FAVORITE MOMENT OF THE TRIP

DATE- MODE OF TRANSPORTATION

THIS IS WHERE WE WENT!

WHERE WE SLEPT

WHO WE MET

DETAILS WORTH REMEMBERING

EXPERIENCES WE CAN'T FORGET

WHAT WE ATE

FAVORITE MOMENT OF THE TRIP

"One's Destination is never a place, but a new way of seeing things." Henry Miller

DETAILS WORTH REMEMBERING

EXPERIENCES WE CAN'T FORGET

WHAT WE ATE

FAVORITE MOMENT OF THE TRIP

DATE- MODE OF TRANSPORTATION

THIS IS WHERE WE WENT!

WHERE WE SLEPT

WHO WE MET

DETAILS WORTH REMEMBERING

EXPERIENCES WE CAN'T FORGET

WHAT WE ATE

FAVORITE MOMENT OF THE TRIP

DATE- MODE OF TRANSPORTATION

THIS IS WHERE WE WENT!

WHERE WE SLEPT

WHO WE MET

DATE- MODE OF TRANSPORTATION

THIS IS WHERE WE WENT!

WHERE WE SLEPT

WHO WE MET

DETAILS WORTH REMEMBERING

EXPERIENCES WE CAN'T FORGET

WHAT WE ATE

FAVORITE MOMENT OF THE TRIP

DATE- MODE OF TRANSPORTATION

THIS IS WHERE WE WENT!

WHERE WE SLEPT

WHO WE MET

DETAILS WORTH REMEMBERING

EXPERIENCES WE CAN'T FORGET

WHAT WE ATE

FAVORITE MOMENT OF THE TRIP

DATE- MODE OF TRANSPORTATION

THIS IS WHERE WE WENT!

WHERE WE SLEPT

WHO WE MET

DETAILS WORTH REMEMBERING

EXPERIENCES WE CAN'T FORGET

WHAT WE ATE

FAVORITE MOMENT OF THE TRIP

"A GOOD TRAVELER HAS
NO FIXED PLANS, AND
IS NOT INTENT ON
ARRIVING."
LAO TZU

DETAILS WORTH REMEMBERING

EXPERIENCES WE CAN'T FORGET

WHAT WE ATE

FAVORITE MOMENT OF THE TRIP

DATE- MODE OF TRANSPORTATION

THIS IS WHERE WE WENT!

WHERE WE SLEPT

WHO WE MET

DETAILS WORTH REMEMBERING

EXPERIENCES WE CAN'T FORGET

WHAT WE ATE

FAVORITE MOMENT OF THE TRIP

DATE- MODE OF TRANSPORTATION

THIS IS WHERE WE WENT!

WHERE WE SLEPT

WHO WE MET

DATE- MODE OF TRANSPORTATION

THIS IS WHERE WE WENT!

WHERE WE SLEPT

WHO WE MET

DETAILS WORTH REMEMBERING

EXPERIENCES WE CAN'T FORGET

WHAT WE ATE

FAVORITE MOMENT OF THE TRIP

DATE- MODE OF TRANSPORTATION

THIS IS WHERE WE WENT!

WHERE WE SLEPT

WHO WE MET

DETAILS WORTH REMEMBERING

EXPERIENCES WE CAN'T FORGET

WHAT WE ATE

FAVORITE MOMENT OF THE TRIP

DATE- MODE OF TRANSPORTATION

THIS IS WHERE WE WENT!

WHERE WE SLEPT

WHO WE MET

DETAILS WORTH REMEMBERING

EXPERIENCES WE CAN'T FORGET

WHAT WE ATE

FAVORITE MOMENT OF THE TRIP

"THE TRAVELER SEES
WHAT HE SEES, THE
TOURIST SEES WHAT HE
HAS COME TO SEE."
G.K. CHESTERTON

LIST OF ALL THE COUNTRIES
IN THE WORLD

A
AFGHANISTAN
ALBANIA
ALGERIA
ANDORRA
ANGOLA
ANTIGUA AND BARBUDA
ARGENTINA
ARMENIA
ARUBA
AUSTRALIA
AUSTRIA
AZERBAIJAN
B
BAHAMAS, THE
BAHRAIN
BANGLADESH
BARBADOS
BELARUS
BELGIUM
BELIZE
BENIN
BHUTAN
BOLIVIA
BOSNIA AND HERZEGOVINA
BOTSWANA
BRAZIL
BRUNEI
BULGARIA
BURKINA FASO
BURMA
BURUNDI

C

CAMBODIA

CAMEROON

CANADA

CABO VERDE

CENTRAL AFRICAN
REPUBLIC

CHAD

CHILE

CHINA

COLOMBIA

COMOROS

CONGO, DEMOCRATIC
REPUBLIC OF THE

CONGO, REPUBLIC OF THE

COSTA RICA

COTE D'IVOIRE

CROATIA

CUBA

CURACAO

CYPRUS

CZECHIA

D

DENMARK

DJIBOUTI

DOMINICA

DOMINICAN REPUBLIC

E

EAST TIMOR SEE TIMOR-
LESTE

ECUADOR

EGYPT

EL SALVADOR

EQUATORIAL GUINEA

ERITREA

ESTONIA

ETHIOPIA

F
FIJI
FINLAND
FRANCE
G
GABON
GAMBIA THE
GEORGIA
GERMANY
GHANA
GREECE
GRENADA
GUATEMALA
GUINEA
GUINEA-BISSAU
GUYANA
H
HAITI
HOLY SEE
HONDURAS
HONG KONG
HUNGARY
I
ICELAND
INDIA
INDONESIA
IRAN
IRAQ
IRELAND
ISRAEL
ITALY
J
JAMAICA
JAPAN
JORDAN
K
KAZAKHTAN
KENYA

K

KIRIBATI
KOREA, NORTH
KOREA, SOUTH
KOSOVO
KUWAIT
KYRGYZSTAN

L

LAOS
LATVIA
LEBANON
LESOTHO
LIBERIA
LIBYA
LIECHTENSTEIN
LITHUANIA
LUXEMBOURG

M

MACAU
MACEDONIA
MADAGASCAR
MALAWI
MALAYSIA
MALDIVES
MALI
MALTA
MARSHALL ISLANDS
MAURITANIA
MAURITIUS
MEXICO
MICRONESIA
MOLDOVA
MONACO
MONGOLIA
MONTENEGRO
MOROCCO
MOZAMBIQUE

N

NAMIBIA

NAURU

NEPAL

NETHERLANDS

NEW ZEALAND

NICARAGUA

NIGER

NIGERIA

NORTH KOREA

NORWAY

O

OMAN

P

PAKISTAN

PALAU

PALESTINIAN TERRITORIES

PANAMA

PAPUA NEW GUINEA

PARAGUAY

PERU

PHILIPPINES

POLAND

PORTUGAL

Q

QATAR

R

ROMANIA

RUSSIA

RWANDA

S

SAINT KITTS AND NEVIS

SAINT LUCIA

SAINT VINCENT AND THE
GRENADINES

SAMOA

S

SAO TOME AND PRINCIPE

SAUDI ARABIA

SENEGAL

SERBIA

SEYCHELLES

SIERRA LEONE

SINGAPORE

SINT MAARTEN

SLOVAKIA

SLOVENIA

SOLOMON ISLANDS

SOMALIA

SOUTH AFRICA

SOUTH KOREA

SOUTH SUDAN

SPAIN

SRI LANKA

SUDAN

SURINAME

SWAZILAND

SWEDEN

SWITZERLAND

SYRIA

T

TAIWAN

TAJIKISTAN

TANZANIA

THAILAND

TIMOR-LESTE

TOGO

TONGA

TRINIDAD AND TOBAGO

TUNISIA

TURKEY

TURKMENISTAN

TUVALU

U
UGANDA
UKRAINE
UNITED ARAB EMIRATES
UNITED KINGDOM
URUGUAY
UZBEKISTAN
V
VANUATU
VENEZUELA
VIETNAM

Y
YEMEN
Z
ZAMBIA
ZIMBABWE

CIRCLE THE COUNTRIES YOU WANT TO VISIT.
LOOK UP THE ONES YOU NEVER HEARD OF.
PICK ONE COUNTRY THAT IS THE
ROAD LESS TRAVELED AND HAVE AN ADVENTURE OF A
LIFETIME.

THE LIST OF COUNTRIES CAN DIFFER FROM DIFFERENT
SOURCES. THIS LIST IS FROM

THE U.S. DEPARTMENT OF STATE.
HTTPS WWW.STATE.GOV MISC LIST INDEX.HTM

DETAILS WORTH REMEMBERING

EXPERIENCES WE CAN'T FORGET

WHAT WE ATE

FAVORITE MOMENT OF THE TRIP

DATE- MODE OF TRANSPORTATION

THIS IS WHERE WE WENT!

WHERE WE SLEPT

WHO WE MET

TRAVEL WISH LIST

TRAVEL WISH LIST

TRAVEL WISH LIST

CHECK OUT OTHER GIFT BOOKS AND JOURNALS
AMAZON.COM AUTHOR BOOKSWITHSOUL
OR GO TO BOOKSWITHSOUL.COM

WHEN WE WERE ONE..PREGNANCY JOURNAL
OLD SOUL NOTEBOOK OF IDEAS FROM AN OLD SOUL
SERIOUSLY YOUR 50?
GRATITUDE JOURNAL I CAN ONLY IMAGINE
MY FUTURE JOURNAL POSSIBILITIES
POSITIVITY JOURNAL JUST BREATH
BOOKS WITH SOUL ANNIVERSARY SERIES
EVERY BREATH A JOURNAL OF GRATITUDE & POSSIBILITIES
MUSIC JOURNAL MY MUSIC JOURNEY
HUNTING SEASON LOG BOOK FACT OR FICTION
UNICORNS ARE REAL STORY NOTEBOOK SERIES
BABY SHARKS ARE REAL STORY NOTEBOOK SERIES
REFLECTIONS FROM THE BEACH